10 **Haight Ashbury** The Summer of Love is now just a memory, but the tie-die shops, tattoo parlors and bars and cafés still draw throngs of dreadlocked youths. **F10**

12 **The ferry to Sausalito** It's worth braving the rough bay waters for a trip to quaint Sausalito. The waterside town is upscale, glossy, and runs on a slower clock than San Francisco. Board at Ferry Building **S4** or Pier 41 **N1**

13 **Bay to Breakers Foot Race** Part serious running race, part mad dash in funny costume, this annual event, held the third Sunday in May, draws thousands of people to the streets. The route stretches from the Ferry Building to Ocean Beach.

14 **The Presidio** You could easily get lost in the hidden trails that wind around this chunk of land between downtown and the Golden Gate. Sights include Crissy Field, a 1920s airfield restored as a wildlife protection area. **C2**

15 **Shopping on Union and Chestnut Streets** Take time out from the sights to shop till you drop in the swanky boutiques of Chestnut St, close to the Marina. **H3–J4**

16 **Alcatraz.** Former fort and jailhouse, now one of the city's top tourist attractions. Put yourself in solitary confinement. **E1**

17 **Coit Tower** This structure is meant to represent the nozzle of a fire hose, and was dedicated to the firemen who lost their lives in the 1906 earthquake. Spectacular views from the top. **P3**

18 **Coffee in North Beach** The beachfront property is long gone, but 'Little Italy' maintains some of the best restaurants and cafes in the city. **P4**

19 **Golden Gate Park** On sunny weekends, San Franciscans abandon the pavement and cram into this three-mile long park, with its gardens, buffalo paddock, an aquarium, and many excellent museums. **B3**

20 **The Castro.** take a historic streetcar to the San Francisco gay community's historic heart, with a great selection of cafés, alternative bookstores, bars and clubs. **X3**

San Francisco

THE ROUGH GUIDE MA

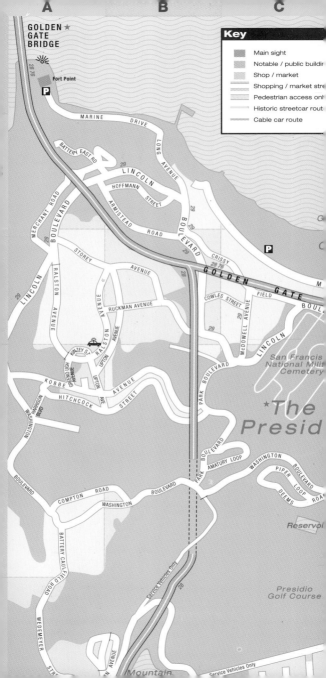

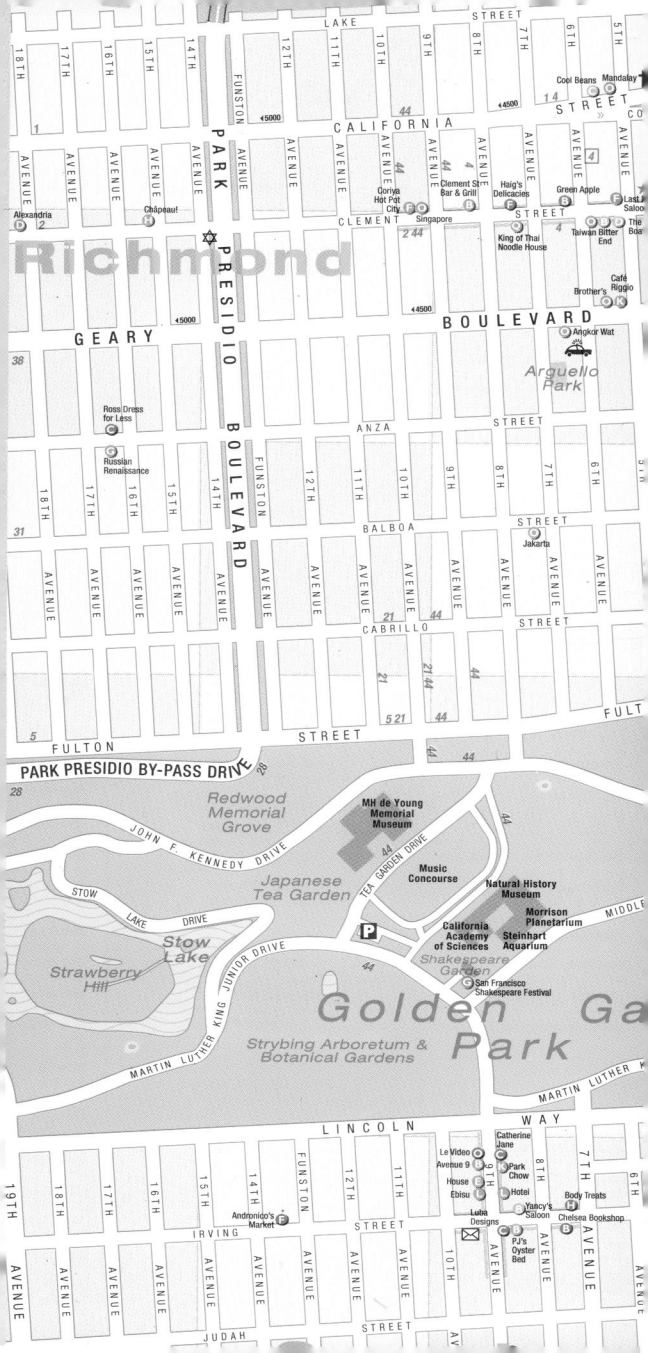

Time Map

Useful opening hours: ■ Open ▢ Seasonal extended opening *with dates*

	TIMES	DAYS

	AM 6 7 8 9 10 11 12 PM 1 2 3 4 5 6 7 8 9 10 11 12 AM 1 2	DAYS
Businesses, Tourist Info		
San Francisco Convention & Visitors Bureau		Mon–Fri
San Francisco Visitor Information Centre P7		Mon–Fri
Post Offices		Mon–Fri / Sat
Banks		Mon–Thu
Sights & Attractions		
Alcatraz E1 (ferries from N1)		Mon–Sun
Ansel Adams Center for Photography Q7		Mon–Sun
Cable Car Museum & Powerhouse N5		Mon–Sun
California Academy of Sciences	*Summer*	Mon–Sun
California Historical Society R6		Tue–Sat
Cartoon Art Museum P7		Mon–Fri / Sat / Sun
Chinese Cultural Centre Q5		Tue–Sun
Chinese Historical Society of America Q5		Tue–Fri
City Lights Bookstore P4		Sat–Thu / Fri–Sat
Cliff House A3		Mon–Thu / Fri–Sun
Coit Tower P3		Mon–Sun
Embarcadero Centre R5		Mon–Sun
Exploratorium F3	*Summer* / *All year* / *Winter*	Thur–Tue / Wed / Tue–Thu & Sur
Fort Point National Historic Site A1		Wed & Sun
Grace Cathedral N5		Sun–Fri / Sat
Haas-Lilienthal House L5		Wed & Sun
Hyde Street Pier L1		Mon–Sun
Japanese Tea Garden B10		Mon–Sun
Jewish Museum of San Francisco S5		Mon–Wed & Su / Thu
Kabuki Hot Springs J7		Mon–Fri / Sat–Sun
Maritime Museum L2		Mon–Sun
Mexican Museum K2		Wed–Fri / Sat–Sun
M.H. de Young Museum B10		Wed–Sun
Mission Dolores K12		Mon–Sun
Museo Italo-Americano J2		Wed–Sun
Musée Méchanique A3		Mon–Fri / Sat–Sun
Museum of Craft & Folk Art J1		Tue–Fri & Sun / Sat

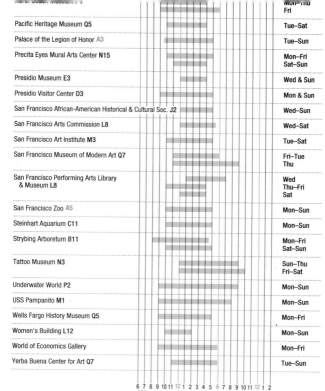

	Hours	Days
North Beach Museum F4		Mon–Thu Fri
Pacific Heritage Museum Q5		Tue–Sat
Palace of the Legion of Honor A3		Tue–Sun
Precita Eyes Mural Arts Center N15		Mon–Fri Sat–Sun
Presidio Museum E3		Wed & Sun
Presidio Visitor Center D3		Mon & Sun
San Francisco African-American Historical & Cultural Soc. J2		Wed–Sun
San Francisco Arts Commission L8		Wed–Sat
San Francisco Art Institute M3		Tue–Sat
San Francisco Museum of Modern Art Q7		Fri–Tue Thu
San Francisco Performing Arts Library & Museum L8		Wed Thu–Fri Sat
San Francisco Zoo A5		Mon–Sun
Steinhart Aquarium C11		Mon–Sun
Strybing Arboretum B11		Mon–Fri Sat–Sun
Tattoo Museum N3		Sun–Thu Fri–Sat
Underwater World P2		Mon–Sun
USS Pampanito M1		Mon–Sun
Wells Fargo History Museum Q5		Mon–Fri
Women's Building L12		Mon–Sun
World of Economics Gallery		Mon–Fri
Yerba Buena Center for Art Q7		Tue–Sun

6 7 8 9 10 11 12 1 2 3 4 5 6 7 8 9 10 11 12 1 2
AM · PM · AM

Red grid references refer to this side of the sheet, black to overleaf.

Venues

All telephone numbers are in the 415 area. **L** Open late ★Highly recommended. Red card references refer to this side of the sheet, black to overleaf. Price symbols indicate the cost of three courses, excluding wine, tax and tip. ● Budget (under $10) ●● Inexpensive ($11–$20) ●●● Moderate ($21–$45) ●●●● Expensive (over $45).

Produced by: Draughtsman Ltd
London W10 5PH Tel:
020-8960 1602:
maps@magneticnorth.net
© Draughtsman Ltd 2002

Cartography by: Dominic Beddow,
Simonetta Giori, Alka Ranger.
Editorial content: Rough Guides

Covers printed by: Forms Technology
(International) Ltd, UK
Map printed by: Victoria Litho Ltd, UK

Draughtsman would like to thank Departure
Lounge and Lisa Kosky for their help and
assistance on this project.

ISBN: 1-84353-002-3

First Edition published April 2002
by Rough Guides Ltd, 62–70 Shorts Gardens,
London WC2H 9AH.

No part of this map may be reproduced in any
form without permission from the publisher.

A catalogue record for this map is available
from the British Library.

The publishers and the cartographers have
done their best to ensure the accuracy and
currency of all information in The Rough
Guide Map of San Francisco; however, they can
accept no responsibility for any loss, injury, or
inconvenience sustained by any traveller as a
result of information or advice on this map.

Distributed by the Penguin Group:
Penguin Books Ltd, 80 The Strand,
London WC2R 0RL, UK

Penguin Putnam, Inc. 375 Hudson Street,
New York, NY 10014, USA

Penguin Books Australia Ltd,
487 Maroondah Highway, PO Box 257,
Ringwood, Victoria 3134, Australia

Penguin Books Canada Ltd,
10 Alcorn Avenue, Toronto, Ontario M4V 1E4,
Canada

Penguin Books (NZ) Ltd,
182–190 Wairau Road, Auckland 10,
New Zealand

Infusion Bar-restaurant 🕿 *543-2282*	S8	
International Italian 🕿		
Pancakes Late-night diner L *921-4004*	L2	
Iron Horse 🕿 *362-8133*	N14	
Izzy's Steaks & Chops 🕿 *563-0487*	L1	
John's Grill 🕿 *986-0669*	M15	
Johnfrank 🕿 *503-0333*	R11	
Just for You Breakfast 🕿 *847-3033*	K12	
Kate's Kitchen 🕿 *626-3984*	G5	
Lori's Late-night diner L 🕿 *921-3039*	L14	
Louis' Diner 🕿 *387-6330*	A3	
MacArthur Park 🕿 *398-5700*	Q9	
Mad Dog in the Fog 🕿 *626-7279*	P5	
Magnolia Brewpub 🕿 *864-PINT*	F5	
Mel's Diner L 🕿 *921-3039* ★	E8, L7, M2	
Orphan Andy's 24 hour L 🕿 *864-9795*	L14	
Pine Crest Diner 🕿 *566-7775*	L14	
PJ's Oyster Bed 🕿 *566-7775*	C12	
Pork Store Coffee Shop 🕿 *864-6981*	M5	
Powell's Soul Food 🕿 *863-1404*	N3	
Q Southern-style 🕿 *752-2298*	D8	
Red's Java House 🕿 *none*	T6	
Rosamunde Sausage		
Grille 🕿 *437-6851*	P5	
Sears Fine Food Breakfast 🕿 *986-1160*	L13	
Sparky's 24 hour L 🕿 *621-6001*	K11	
Swan Oyster Depot		
Seafood 🕿 *673-1101* ★	L6	
Tadich Grill 🕿 *391-1849*	Q11	
Tita's Hale Aina Hawaiian 🕿 *626-2477*	E14	
Tommy's Joynt 🕿 *775-4216*	L7	
Yabbie's Seafood 🕿 *474-4088*	L4	
Zare 🕿 *861-8868*	L5	

B Brazilian

Café do Brasil 🕿 *626-6432*	N8	
Terra Brazilis 🕿 *241-1900*	N3	

C Cajun

Belle Roux 🕿 *771-5225*	M2	
Elite Café 🕿 *346-8668* ★	L4	

E Californian

2223 🕿 *431-0692*	F13	
42 Degrees Supper Club 🕿 *777-5558*	T11	
Asia SF Drag review 🕿 *255-2742* ★	N9	
Asqew Grill 🕿 *701-9301*	L5	
Betelnut 🕿 *929-8855*	P1	
California Culinary		
Academy 🕿 *771-3500*	M8	
Citizen Cake Desserts 🕿 *861-2228*	P3	
Cypress Club Stylee 🕿 *296-8555*	N9	
Ella's 🕿 *441-5669*	S2	
EOS 🕿 *566-3063*	F12	
Fifth Floor Seafood *956-6969*	L13	
Firefth Floor 🕿 *348-1555*	N15	
Flying Saucer 🕿 *641-9955*	G16	
Globe 🕿 *391-4132*	Q9	
Hayes Street Grill 🕿 *863-5545*	N13	
House Fusion 🕿 *682-3898*	C12	
Indigo 🕿 *673-9369*	L8	
Jardinière 🕿 *861-5555* ★	L3	
Julie's Supper Club 🕿 *861-0707*	P9	
Lulu 🕿 *495-5775*	Q8	
mc2 🕿 *956-0666*	P8	
McKormick & Kuleto's		
Fish 🕿 *929-1730*	L2	
Mecca Supper Club 🕿 *621-7000*	K14	
Millennium Vegan 🕿 *487-9800*	M8	
Miss Millie's 🕿 *282-5598*	J15	
Oritalia Fusion 🕿 *346-1333*	M7	

A Other European

Kokkari Estiatorio Greek 🕿 *981-0983* ★	Q9	
Martin Mack's British *864-0124*	L5	
Moishe's Pipic Jewish deli 🕿 *431-2440*	P3	
Traktir Russian 🕿 *386-9800*	A3	
Russian Renaissance 🕿 *752-8558*	A9	
Schroeders German 🕿 *421-4778*	N3	
Suppenküche German 🕿 *252-9289*	N3	

H French

Absinthe 🕿 *551-1590*	P3	
Bizou Bistro 🕿 *543-2222* ★	R9	
Café Bastille 🕿 *986-5673*	P12	
Café Claude 🕿 *392-3505*	N13	
Café Mozart 🕿 *391-8480*	L12	
Châpeau! 🕿 *750-9787*	A8	
Charles Nob Hill 🕿 *771-5400* ★	N5	
Clementine 🕿 *387-0408*	D7	
Crêpes on Cole 🕿 *664-1800*	F11	
Des Alpes Basque 🕿 *391-4249*	L9	
Fleur de Lys 🕿 *673-7779*	K13	
La Folie Lyonnaise 🕿 *776-5577*	L4	
Grand Café 🕿 *441-8080*	K14	
Jeanne d'Arc 🕿 *421-3154*	L13	
Ma Tante Sumi Japanese fusion		
🕿 *552-6663*	D15	
Masa's 🕿 *989-7154*	L12	
Matterhorn Fondue 🕿 *885-6116*	L4	
Moose's 🕿 *989-7800*	P3	
Pastis 🕿 *391-2555*	P7	
Piaf's 🕿 *864-3700*	L10	
Plouf Provençal seafood 🕿 *986-6491*	N12	
South Park Café Bistro 🕿 *495-7275*	R8	
Ti Couz Breton 🕿 *252-7373* ★	G13	

I Indian

The Ganges Vegetarian 🕿 *661-7290*	E12	
Indian Oven 🕿 *626-1628*	O5	
Rasoi 🕿 *695-0599*	H15	
Shalimar 🕿 *928-0333*	K14	

K Italian

Albona Ristorante		
Istriano North Italian 🕿 *441-1040*	N2	
Black Cat 🕿 *981-2233*	N9	
Blondie's Pizza 🕿 *982-6168*	L15	
Buca di Beppo 🕿 *543-7673*	Q8	
Café Macaroni 🕿 *956-9737*	N10	
Café Riggio 🕿 *221-2114*	C8	
Café Tiramisu 🕿 *421-7044*	P12	
Caffé Delle Stelle 🕿 *986-2674*	P3	
Capp's Corner 🕿 *989-2589*	K8	
Chow 🕿 *552-2469*	K11	
Club Za Pizza 🕿 *552-5599*	N10	
Delfina 🕿 *552-4055* ★	L13	
Enrico's 🕿 *982-6223*	M8	
Escape from New York		
Pizza 🕿 *252-1515*	D15	
Fior d'Italia 🕿 *986-1886*	L7	
The Gold Spike 🕿 *986-9747*	K8	
Golden Boy Pizza 🕿 *982-9738*	M8	
Il Massimo del Panino 🕿 *834-0290*	P10	
Il Polliao 🕿 *362-7727*	L8	
Jackson Fillmore 🕿 *346-5288*	J5	
Kuleto's Pasta 🕿 *397-7720*	L14	
Little City 🕿 *434-2900*	K7	
Little Joe's 🕿 *433-4343*	M9	
Marcello's Pizza 🕿 *863-3900*	D14	
Maye's Oyster House 🕿 *474-7674*	L6	
Michelangelo's 🕿 *986-4058*	L8	

M Mexican

Andale Chain 🕿 *749-0506*	L1	
Café Marimba 🕿 *778-1506*	K2	
Chava's 🕿 *552-9387*	M12	
El Balazo 🕿 *864-8608*	L5	
Panchita's 🕿 *431-4232*	G13	
Pancho Villa 🕿 *864-8840*	G13	
Roosevelt Tamale Parlor 🕿 *550-9213*	P15	
La Taqueria 🕿 *285-7117*	M15	
Taqueria Cancun 🕿 *252-9560*	M13	
Tommy's 🕿 *387-4747*	B3	
Zona Rosa 🕿 *668-7717*	K6	

N Middle Eastern

Kan Zaman Belly dancers 🕿 *751-9656*	K6	
La Méditerranée 🕿 *921-2956*	L3	
Truly Mediterranean 🕿 *252-7482*	G13	

O Other Oriental

Angkor Wat Cambodian 🕿 *221-7887*	C8	
Borobudur Indonesian 🕿 *775-1512*	J14	
Brother's Korean 🕿 *387-3991*	C8	
Irrawaddy Burmese 🕿 *931-2830*	K3	
Jakarta Indonesian 🕿 *387-5225*	C9	
Lhasa Moon Tibetan 🕿 *674-9898*	K2	
Mandalay Burmese 🕿 *386-3895*	C7	
Singapore Malaysian 🕿 *750-9518*	B8	
Straits Café Singaporean 🕿 *668-1783*	E8	
Taiwan Taiwanese 🕿 *387-1789*	C8	

P Spanish

Cha Cha Cha 🕿 *386-5758* ★	K6	
Esperpento 🕿 *642-8867*	H16	
Thirsty Bear Brewing		
Company 🕿 *974-0905*	Q15	
Timo's Tapas 🕿 *647-0558*	L13	

Q Thai

Khan Toke 🕿 *668-6654*	B3	
King of Thai Noodle		
House 🕿 *752-5198*	C8	
Manora 🕿 *861-6224*	M10	
Marnee Thai 🕿 *665-9500*	B4	
Slanted Door Vietnamese		
dishes 🕿 *861-8032* ★	G14	
Thai House 🕿 *863-0374*	J11	
Thep Phanom 🕿 *431-2526*	P6	

R Vegetarian

Herbivore Vegan 🕿 *826-5657*	G15	
Firefly Veggie options 🕿 *821-7652*	H15	
Greens 🕿 *771-6222* ★	J2	
Kowloon Chinese 🕿 *362-9888*	M10	
Lotus Garden Vegetarian 🕿 *982-3656.*	N12	
Lucky Creation Vegetarian 🕿 *989-0818*	M10	
Millennium Vegan 🕿 *487-9800*	M8	
The Ganges Indian 🕿 *661-7290*	E12	
Yoshi-san's Monkichi Sushi: veggie		
options 🕿 *876-1834*	B3	

S Vietnamese

Le Colonial 🕿 *931-3600*	K14	
The Golden Turtle 🕿 *441-4419*	L4	
Hung Yen 🕿 *621-8531*	N12	
Tu Lan 🕿 *626-0927*	N8	
La Vie 🕿 *668-8080*	B3	
Vietnam II 🕿 *885-1274*	M7	

Drinking

B Bar

111 Minna Art Gallery	Q14	
The Albion	G13	
An Bodhran Irish / Live music	M7	
Backflip	M7	
Balboa Café Singles	M2	
Bar on Castro	D14	
The Big Four (in hotel)	K12	
Bitter End Irish	B3	
Blarney Stone Irish	B3	
Bobby's Owl Tree Irish	L13	
Bubble Lounge Champagne ★	N10	
Buddha Bar Lounge	M10	
Butter	N10	
Café Flore	E13	
The Caribbean Zone	R6	
Carnelian Room Rooftop	N11	
Casanova	G13	
Cathay House	M11	
Club Deluxe	M5	
Compass Rose (in hotel)	L14	
The Crow Bar Dive	N9	
Dalva	G13	
Detour Gay	E14	
E&O Trading Company		
Brewpub & restaurant	M13	
Eastside West Singles	M2	
Edinburgh Castle Fish & chips	M7	

Harry Denton's Starlight		
Room Rooftop ★	M13	
Harry's on Fillmore Blues	L4	
Harvey's	N14	
Hawaii West	L8	
Hayes and Vine Wine	L3	
Hole in the Wall		
Saloon Biker bar	N9	
House of Shields	P14	
John Barleycorn	L8	
Kimo's Drag	L6	
Latin American Club	L13	
Lexington Club Lesbian	L13	
Li Po's Bar	M10	
The London Wine Bar	P11	
The Lone Palm Cocktail	G15	
The Lone Star Gay	K11	
Lucky 13 Rock	E13	
Mad Dog in the Fog British	P5	
Marlena's Drag	M5	
Martin Macks British	L5	
Martuni's Gay	L3	
Midnight Sun Gay	E13	
Molotov	K10	
The Motherlode Transvestite	L14	
My Place Gay	N9	
Noc Noc	O5	

POW!	P8	
Powerhouse Gay	N10	
The Ramp	T16	
Red Room Lounge ★	J14	
The Redwood Room (in hotel)	K14	
La Rondalla Mariachi music	G14	
Royal Exchange	Q11	
San Francisco Brewing		
Company Brewpub	M9	
Savoy Tivoli ★	M8	
The SF Eagle Leather bar	N10	
Silver Cloud	J3	
Spec's	M9	
Tonga Room Theme ★	L12	
Top of the Mark Rooftop	L12	
Tosca Café	M9	
Trad'r Sam's Theme	B3	
Trapdoor Singles	K2	
Trax Gay	N10	
Twenty Tank	N10	
Twin Peaks Gay	D14	
Vesuvio Cafe ★	M9	
View Lounge Rooftop	N15	
Yancy's Saloon Studenty	C12	
Zeitgeist Biker	L10	
Zero Degrees Cafe-bar	N9	

C Café

Cool Beans Chess &		
backgammon	C7	
Farley's	R12	
Horseshoe Café	P5	
Imperial Tea Court	K9	
Java Beach Café	A4	
Lovejoy's Tea shop	K15	
Mario's Bohemian		
Cigar Store	L7	
Momi Toby's Revolutionary		
Café Board games	N4	
Mr Ralph's Café	R6	
Pendragon	P3	
People's Café	M5	
Primo Patio	S8	
Red Dora's Bearded		
Lady Lesbian	L11	
South Beach Café	T8	
Squat and Gobble	P5	
Stella Pastry	L8	
Steps of Rome Café	M8	
Tosca Café	M9	
Yakety Yak	K13	

D Ice Cream Parlor

St. Francis Fountain 50s style	P15	
Swenson's Ice Cream	M4	
The Toy Boat	C8	

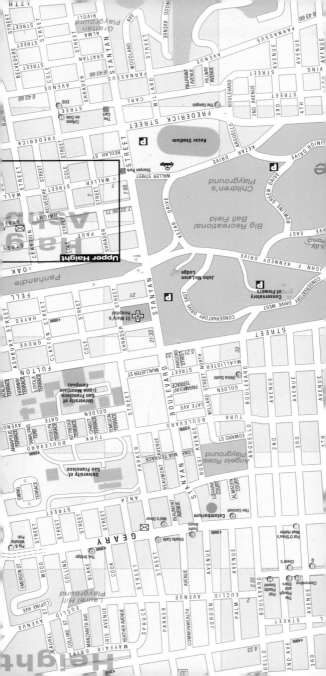

Recommendations

Listings below are all recommended in the Rough Guide book - and all are shown on this map. The ones we like best are starred.

Shopping

Ⓐ Antiques

Antonio's Antiques	Q9
Asakichi	J7
Biordi	M8
Genji	K7

Ⓑ Books

A Clean, Well Lighted Place for Books	M8
A Different Light Gay/Lesbian	E15
Aardvark Books Secondhand	D15
Acorn Books Secondhand	M6
Around the World Secondhand	M6
Black Oak Books Secondhand	M8
The Booksmith	L5
Borders Books and Music	L13
Bound Together Anarchist Collective Bookstore Politics	N5
Chelsea Bookshop Secondhand	C12
China Books Politics	P15
City Lights Bookstore ★	M9
Fields Bookstore New Age	L6
Good Vibrations Sex	M14
Great Expectations Politics	L5
Green Apple	L5
Kinokuniya Japanese	J7
The Maritime Store	L4
Modern Times Gay & Lesbian	L13
Phoenix Books and Records Secondhand	K15
Rand McNally Map & Travel Store Travel	Q13
Russian Hill Bookstore Secondhand	L4
Sierra Club Bookstore Outdoor	Q13
Stacey's Professional Bookstore Business	Q13
William Stout Architectural Books	P9

Ⓒ Clothes

Aardvark's Odd Ark Secondhand	M5
Agnes b Designer	N14
American Rag Co Secondhand	L6
Backseat Betty Designer	L5
Banana Republic Casual	N13
Bargain Mart Thrift	L6
Betsey Johnson Designer	L4
Bryan Lee Designer	Q1
Buffalo Exchange Secondhand	L5
Catherine Jane Designer	C12
Clothes Contact Secondhand	G13
Community Thrift Thrift	G14

Dema Designer	G15
Departures from the Past Secondhand	L4
Diesel Designer	N13
Emporio Armani Designer	N13
Esprit Casual	T11
The Gap Casual	M15
Groper's Western Wear Casual	M15
Jeremy's Secondhand	S8
Levi's Casual	N13
Loehmann's Secondhand	L13
Luba Designs Designer	C12
Manifesto Designer	N3
Metier Designer	M2
North Beach Leather Casual	N13
Patagonia Casual	M2
Repeat Performance SF	
Symphony Thrift Store Thrift	L3
Retro Fit Vintage Secondhand	D15
Rolo Designer	E14
Ross Dress for Less Thrift	A8
Schauplatz Secondhand	L13
Seconds-To-Go Resale	L6
Shop Thrift	L5
Third Hand Store Secondhand	H7
Utopia Planitia Designer	M12
Villains Casual	L5
Wasteland Casual	L5
Wilkes Bashford Designer	M13

Ⓓ Department Stores & Malls

Crocker Galleria	P13
Embarcadero Center	R5
Ghirardelli Square	L2
Gump's	K7
Japan Center	K7
Macy's Union Square	M14
Nieman Marcus	M16
Nordstrom	N16
Sak's Fifth Avenue	M14
San Francisco Shopping Center	P7
Sony Metreon	P16

Ⓔ Food

Andronico's Market	B12
Bombay Bazar Spices	G13
Boudin Bakery	N2
California Wine Merchant ★	K2
Cannery Wine Cellars	L2
Casa Lucas Delicatessen	P15
The Cheesery Delicatessen	D14
Cigar Liquor Wine	L7
D & M Wine & Liquor Co.	K14
David's Delicatessen	

Farmers Market Saturday	Q7
Godiva Chocolates	M16
Graffeo Coffee	K7
Haig's Delicacies	C7
Harvest Ranch Market ★	E13
Heart of the City Farmer's Market	N8
Italian French Baking Co.	L7
The Jug Shop Wine	L6
Just Desserts Patisserie	K11
Liguria Bakery Focaccia	L7
Lo-Cost Market Delicatessen	P5
Lucca Ravioli Delicatessen	G16
Molinari's Delicatessen	M8
Pasta Gina Delicatessen	C12
Peet's Coffee and Tea	M11
Rainbow Grocery Delicatessen	N11
San Francisco Health Foods Delicatessen	M13
San Francisco Herb Co. ★	M11
Swan Oyster Depot Delicatessen	L6
Sweet Inspirations Patisserie	E13
Urban Cellars Wine	K15
The Wine Club Wine	Q9

Ⓕ Commercial Art Galleries

Art Collective Gallery	E6
Atelier Dore Inc.	L13
The Audium	L6
Bond Latin Gallery	L13
Clarion Alley	G14
Encantada Gallery	N13
Erickson & Elins	N13
Fraenkel Gallery	N14
Galeria de la Raza	P15
Hackett-Freedman Gallery	M13
Japonesque	P9
John Berggruen Gallery	N13
John Pence Gallery	J14
Joseph Chowning Gallery	Q12
Mission Cultural Center	M11
Modernism	P14
New Langton Arts	N9
Rena Bransten Gallery	N14
Ruby Artists Cooperative	N14
San Francisco Art Institute	M3
SF MoMA Artists Gallery	L13
Smile	L3
Vorpal Gallery	N13

Ⓖ Health & Beauty

BeneFit	L4
Body Time	P1
Body Treats	C12
Common Scents	K15

Isa's Hair Studio	K15
Sephora	M15
Skin Zone	E15

Ⓜ Music

Amoeba Records ★	K6
CD & Record Rack	F15
Discolandia	N15
Flat Plastic Sound	D7
Green Apple	C7
Groove Merchant Records	P6
Jack's Record Cellar	J10
Let It Be Records	B4
Medium Rare	E13
Musica Latina	
/American Music Store	L14
Reckless Records	M5
Recycled Records	N5
Rooky Ricardo's	Q5
Streetlight Records	K15
Tower Records	M2
Virgin Megastore	M15

Ⓝ New Age

Psychic Eye	P4

Ⓞ Other

Body Manipulations Piercing, Tattoos	K12
Brooks Cameras Photographic	N13
Cliff's Variety Hardware	E15
Cottage Industry Asian crafts	J15
The Dreaming Room Folk art	M9
FAO Schwarz Toys	M14
Fredericksen Hardware	N1
Lost Weekend Video Video	Q15
Mom's Bodyshop Piercing	M5
Under One Roof Decor	N5
Union Street Papery Stationery	N1
Le Video Video	C12

Ⓢ Shoes & Accessories

China Gem Co.	N12
The Coach Store	N13
Ghurka	N13
Gimme Shoes	N14
Hats on Post	N13
Hermes	M14
Kenneth Cole	N1
Laku	H16
Mapuche	N4
Pearl of the Orient	L2
Shapur	M13
Shreve & Co	N13
Tiffany	M13

Eating

Ⓐ African

Axum Café Ethiopian ● 252-7912	N5
Baobab West African ● 643-3558	M13
Massawa Ethiopian ● 621-4129	L5

Ⓑ American

Aqua Seafood ● 956-9662 ★	Q11
Avenue 9 ● 664-6999	C12
Bagdad Café Diner L. 921-3039	E13
Beach Chalet ● 386-8439	A3
Big Sherm's Sandwich ● 864-1850	Q5
Bistro Aix ● 202-0100	N4
Bitterroot ● 626-5523	G13
Bix Supper club ● 433-6300	P9
Blue ● 863-2583	E14
Boogaloo's Breakfast ● 824-3211	G16
Boulevard ● 563-6084	S5
Café Cuvée ● 775-4300	K11
Café Florio Bistro ● 775-4300	L4
Cheer's ● 387-6966	D8
Clement Street Bar & Grill ●	C7
Cliff House ● 386-3330	A3
Clown Alley ● 421-2540	N10
Delancey Street ● 512-5179	S7
Firefly Veggie options ● 821-7652	H15
Fog City Diner ● 982-2000	Q3
Gordon Biersch ● 392-2696	S6

Pacific Café Fish ● 387-7091	A3
Plumpjack Café ● 563-4755	N2
Postrio ● 776-7825	L14
Sabella's Fish ● 771-6775	M2
Tin Pan ● 565-0733	F13
Waterfront Café ● 391-2696	R4
xyz ● 817-7836	Q15
Zuni ● 552-2522	L10

Ⓒ Chinese

Chef Jia's ● 398-1626	N9
The Citrus Club ● 387-6366	K6
Coriya Hot Pot City ● 387-7888	B7
Dragon Well ● 474-6888	L1
Eliza's ● 621-4819	H6
Empress of China ● 434-1345	M10
Firecracker ● 642-3470	G13
Garden of Tranquility ● 861-8610	Q12
Gold Mountain ● 296-7733	M9
Great Eastern ● 986-2500	N10
Harbor Village ● 781-8833	R5
House of Nanking ● 421-1429	N9
Kowloon Vegetarian ● 362-9888	M10
Long Life Noodle House and Jook Joint ● 281-3818	S5
Lotus Garden Vegetarian ● 982-3656	N12
Lucky Creation Vegetarian ● 989-0818	M10
Pot Sticker Szechuan	

Ⓓ Japanese

Ace Wasabi ● 567-4903	L1
Akiko Sushi ● 397-3218	N12
Blowfish ● 285-3848	P13
Country Station Sushi ● 861-0972	H14
Ebisu Sushi ● 566-1770	C12
Hamano Sushi Sushi ● 826-0825	J15
Hotei ● 753-6045	C9
Isobune Sushi ● 563-1030	J7
Kushi Tsuru Noodle house ● 922-9902	J7
Mifune Noodle house ● 922-0337	K7
Moshi Moshi ● 861-8285	T12
Okina Sushi ● 387-8882	D9
On the Bridge ● 922-7765	J7
Sapporo-ya ● 563-7400	J7
Shiki ● 512-8136	Q15
Sushi Bune Sushi ● 781-5111	L14

Mozzarella di Bufala ● 346-9928	L4
L'Osteria del Forno ● 982-1124	K8
Park Chow ● 665-9912	C12
Pauline's Pizza ● 552-2050	L11
Pizza Orgasmica Pizza ● 931-5300	M2
Rose Pistola ● 399-0499	L8
Stelline ● 626-4292	P3
The Stinking Rose Garlic ● 781-7673	M3
Via Veneto ● 346-9211	L3
Vicolo Pizza ● 863-2382	P7

Key

▢ Main sight	– – – Ferry route	▭101▭ US Highway	
▢ Notable / public building	—— Historic streetcar route	⤳1⤳ State Highway	
▢ Shop / market	—— Cable car route	★ Highly recommended	
▤ Shopping / market street	—— Bus route	▣ Hotel	
▢ Pedestrian access only	*15* Bus number	Ⓐ Restaurant	
† Church	⑦ Bus termini	Ⓑ Bar / pub / café	
✡ Synagogue	🚌 Bus terminal	Ⓒ Entertainment / nightlife venue	
✉ Post office	C Caltrain station	Ⓓ Shop / market	
🚓 Police station	M Muni Metro station	(Letter in dot indicates restaurant, bar, entertainment or shop category in index)	
i Tourist information	—— Muni Metro route		
P Parking	ba BART station		
✚ Hospital	═══ BART route		
🔆 Viewpoint	✈ Airport		
⛴ Ferry	▬280▬ Interstate Highway		

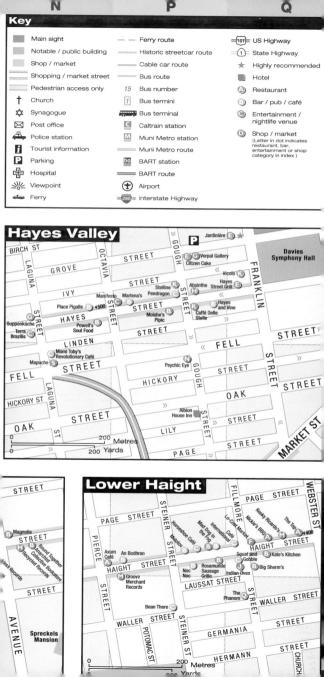

Hayes Valley

Davies Symphony Hall

Jardinière Ⓔ ★

Vorpal Gallery Ⓔ
Citizen Cake Ⓑ

Vicolo Ⓚ

Stelline Ⓔ   Hayes
Pendragon Ⓐ   Street Grill Ⓔ
Manifesto Ⓓ Marlena's Ⓒ Absinthe Ⓗ

Place Pigalle Ⓑ ◄500 Hayes
                    and Vine Ⓚ
Suppenküche Ⓖ   Moishe's
Terra   Pipic Ⓚ   Caffè Delle
Brazilis Ⓖ Powell's   Stelle Ⓙ
            Soul Food Ⓑ

Momi Toby's
Revolutionary Café Ⓢ
Mapuche Ⓢ

Psychic Eye Ⓝ

Albion
House Inn ▣

0 ——— 200 Metres
0 ——— 200 Yards

Lower Haight

Magnolia Ⓑ

Bound Together
Anarchist
Collective Bookstore Ⓓ
Recycled Records Ⓓ

Spreckels
Mansion

Magnolia Ⓑ

Rocky Ricardo's Ⓓ The Top Ⓒ

Mad Dog in   Lo-Cost Market Ⓓ
the Fog Ⓑ

International Ⓑ Nickie's BBQ Ⓒ
Café

Horseshoe Café Ⓑ   ◄400

Axum   An Bodhran Ⓑ Squat and Kate's Kitchen Ⓐ
Café Ⓑ   Gobble Ⓐ

Groove   Noc   Rosamunde Indian Oven Ⓐ Big Sherm's Ⓐ
Merchant   Noc   Sausage
Records Ⓜ   Ⓑ   Grille Ⓑ

Bean There Ⓑ   The
               Phanom Ⓒ

0 ——— 200 Metres
0 ——— Yards

G   H   J

San   Francisco   B

Wave
Organ

Marina Small
Craft Harbor

Museo Italo-
Americano

San Francisco Craft
& Folk Art Museum

SF MoMA Artists Gallery

Greens

West
Harbor

ROAD

MARINA   GREEN   DRIVE

Marina Green

East
Harbor

Fort
Ce

P

P

P

28

G

CASA WAY

RICO WAY

RETIRO WAY

22

JEFFERSON
STREET

WEBSTER

BEACH

BUCHANAN ST

28

28

MARINA

STREET

SCOTT

CERVANTES

PRADO ST

VILLA ST

CASA WAY

STREET

FILLMORE

STREET

NORTH
POINT

STREET

28

28

LAGUNA

30

BEACH

AVILA

PIERCE

MALLORCA

BOULEVARD

STREET

STREET

WAY

STREET

22

Funston
Playground

POINT

BAY

STREET

DIVISADERO

STREET

STREET

CAPRA

WAY

ALHAMBRA

STREET

BOULEVARD

WAY

4 2600

Marina

NCISCO

STREET

STREET

30

30

CHESTNUT

28 43 76

Marina

ALHAMBRA
ST

TOLEDO WAY

STREET

4 2000

43

43

MAGNOLIA   STREET

Silver Cloud

28

Del Sol

STREET

GREENWICH

BUCHANAN

LOMBARD   **STREET**

MOULTON

PIXLEY ST

4 2000

Art Cen

w Hollow

GREENWICH

STREET

STREET

PIERCE

STEINER

Chestnut

4 2000

Vedanta
Temple

Book Time

Union

Betelnut

Blue
Light Café

Cow Hollow
Playground

MILEY
STREET

41 45

FILBERT

4 2500

STREET

4 2500

STREET

Fredericksen
Hardware

Yoshida-Ya

Union
Street
Papery

2040
Union

4 2000

The
Metro

N CHARLTON
COURT

G P

UNION

STREET

**Church of
St Mary
the Virgin**

STEINER

ORR E

WEBSTER

STREET

Sherman
House

WEBSTER

STREET

GREEN

STREET

STREET

4 2500

2222
Broadway
(Convent of the
Sacred Heart
High School)

STEINER

PACIFIC

VALLEJO

NORMANDIE
TERRACE

BROADWAY

BRODERICK

DIVISADERO

AVENUE

SCOTT

Jackson
Fillmore

24

BROMLEY
PLACE

JACKSO

BAKER

STREET

El Drisco

STREET

24

4 2500

4 2500

Pac
Hei

WAST

JACKSON

4 3000

STREET

Alta
Plaza
Park

Pacific Heights

4 2500

24

WEBSTER

ASHINGTON

STREET

4 3000

STREET

STREET

CLAY

4 2500

STREET

4 2500

CLAY

4 3000

STREET

STEINER

FILLMORE

SACRAMENTO

22

4 2500

SACRAMENTO

PERINE PLACE

4 2500

ORBEN
PLACE

4 2000

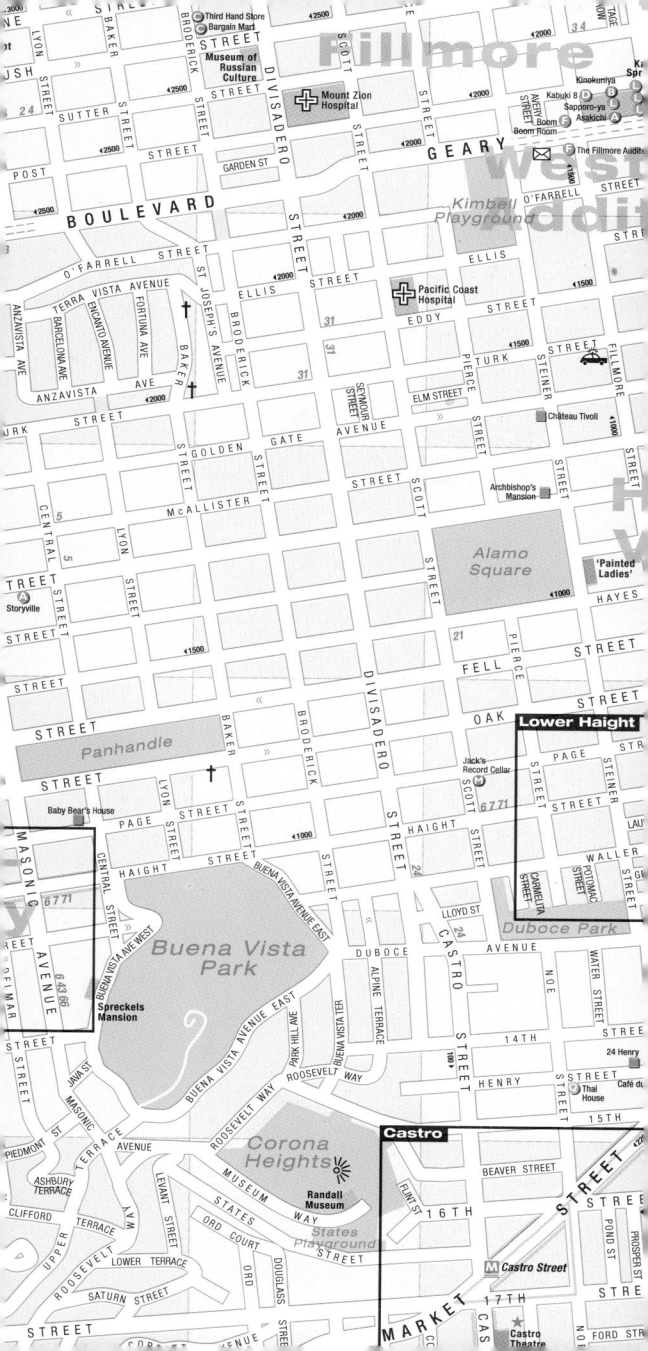

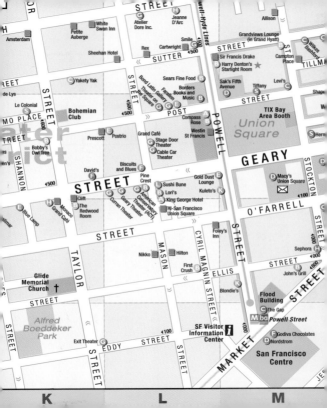

STREET

Amsterdam

Petite
Auberge

White
Swan Inn

Atelier
Dore Inc.

Jeanne
D'Arc

Allison

Grandviews Lounge
(in Grand Hyatt)

STREET

Willies
Bootleg

Sheehan Hotel

Smile

SUTTER

Cartwright

Rex

500

Sir Francis Drake

Campton
Place

TILLM

Yakety Yak

de Lys

Le Colonial

Bohemian
Club

STREET

600

500

Bond Latin Gallery
Farmers
Theater on
the Square

Sears Fine Food

Borders
Books and
Music

POST

Harry Denton's
Starlight Room

Sak's Fifth
Avenue

Tiffany

STREET

Levi's

Shape

W

MO PLACE

Prescott

Postrio

Grand Café

Compass
Rose

Westin
St Francis

POWELL

TIX Bay
Area Booth

Union
Square

Herm

Bobby's
Owl Tree

ater

rict

SHANNON

500

David's

Stage Door
Theater

Cable Car
Theater

GEARY

STOCKTON

Macy's
Union Square

100

Biscuits
and Blues

Pine
Crest

STREET

Sushi Bune

Lori's

King George Hotel

Gold Dust
Lounge

Kuleto's

O'FARRELL

Clift

Morosco
Grand Cafe

The
Redwood
Room

American
Conservatory
Theater (ACT)

Geary Theater

Hl-San Francisco
Union Square

STREET

Sephora

600

Blue Lamp

talmar

en's

TAYLOR

STREET

Foley's
Inn

CYRIL MAGNIN

STREET

John's Grill

Nikko

Hilton

MASON

First
Crush

ELLIS

Blondie's

Flood
Building

The Gap

STREET

Powell Street

Glide
Memorial
Church

STREET

Alfred
Boeddeker
Park

Exit Theater

100

EDDY

STREET

MARKET

SF Visitor
Information
Center

Godiva Chocolates

Nordstrom

San Francisco
Centre

JE

K

L

M

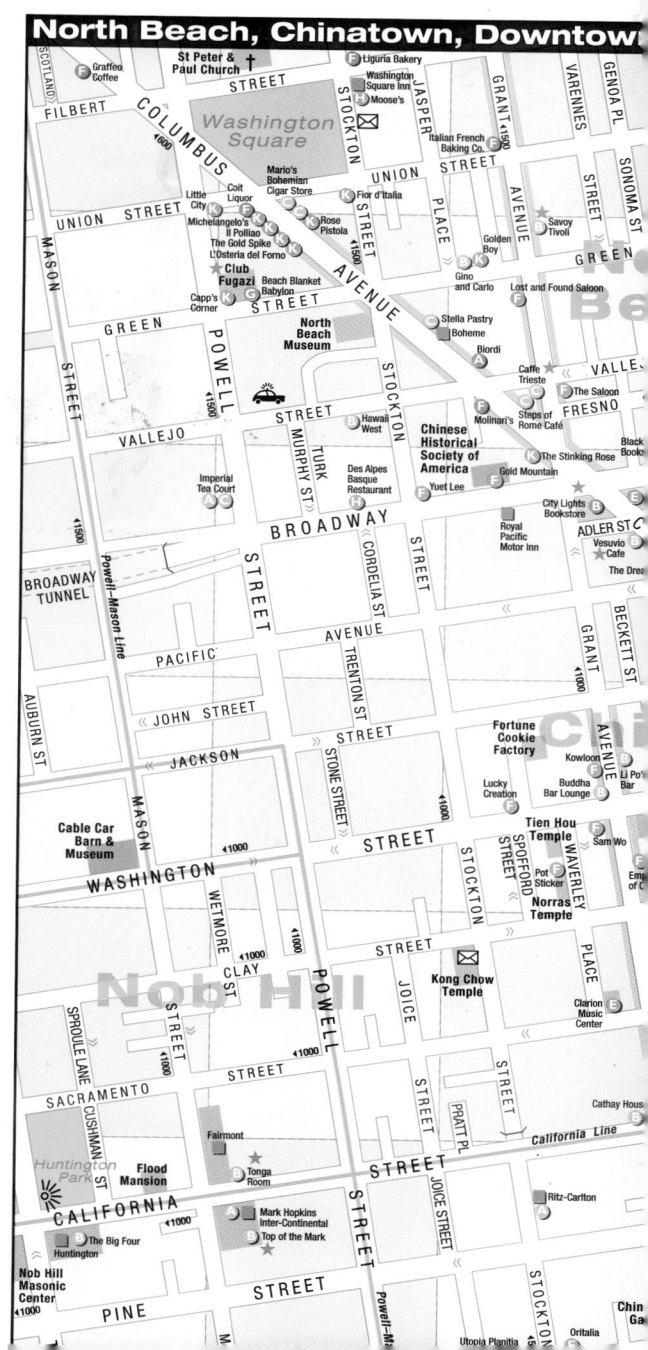

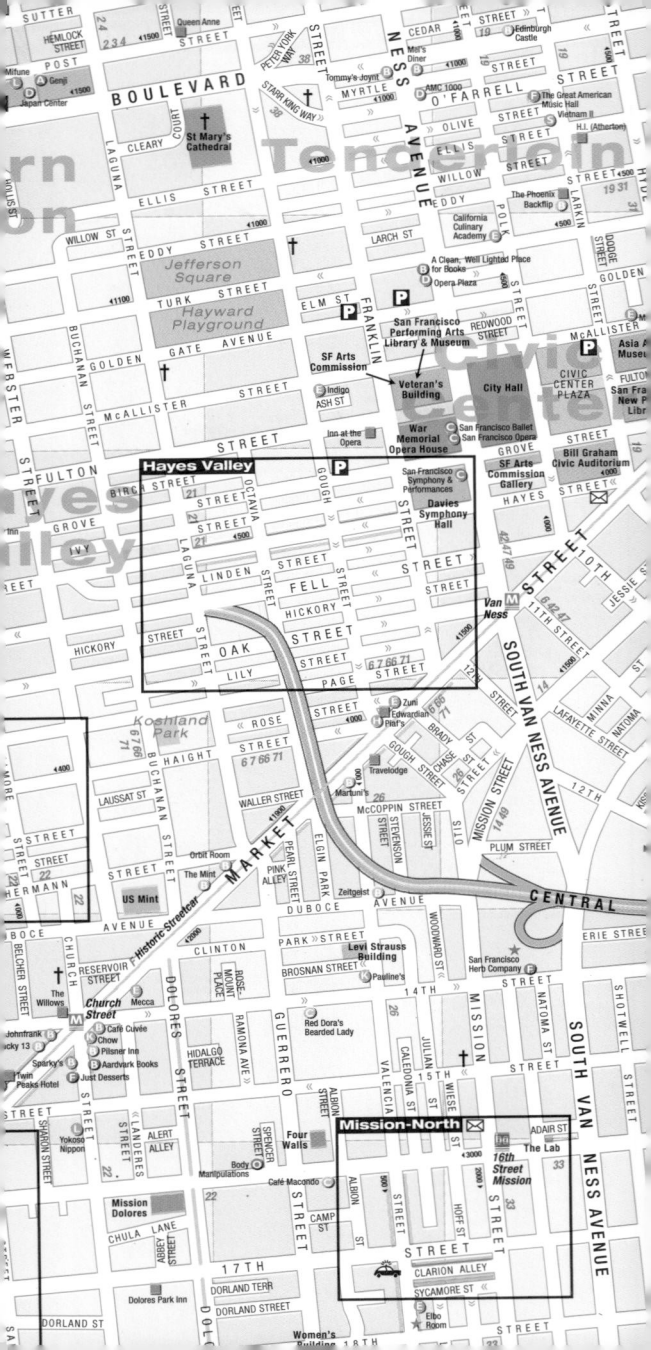

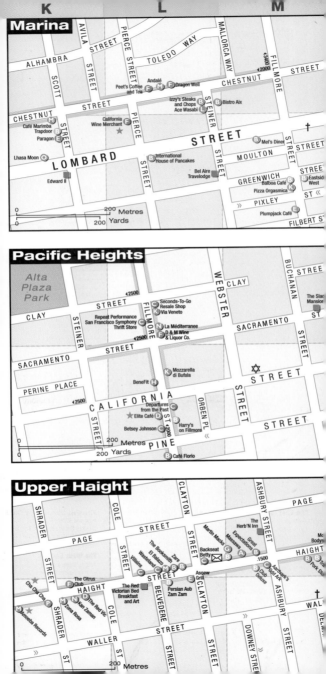

Marina

K — AVILA STREET — PIERCE STREET — TOLEDO WAY — MALLORCA WAY — FILLMORE STREET — **M**

ALHAMBRA STREET

SCOTT STREET

CHESTNUT STREET

Peet's Coffee and Tea
Andalé
Dragon Well
Izzy's Steaks and Chops
Ace Wasabi
Bistro Aix
CHESTNUT STREET

Café Marimba
Trapdoor
Paragon

California Wine Merchant

PIERCE STREET

STREET

Mel's Diner

MOULTON STREET

Lhasa Moon

LOMBARD

Edward II

International House of Pancakes
Bel Aire Travelodge

Balboa Café
GREENWICH

Pizza Orgasmica

Eastsid West

PIXLEY STREET

Plumpjack Café

FILBERT ST

0 — 200 Metres
0 — 200 Yards

Pacific Heights

Alta Plaza Park

CLAY STREET

STEINER STREET

FILLMORE STREET

WEBSTER STREET

CLAY STREET

BUCHANAN STREET

The Slac Mansion

Seconds-To-Go Resale Shop
Via Veneto
Repeat Performance San Francisco Symphony Thrift Store
La Méditerranee
D & M Wine & Liquor Co.

SACRAMENTO STREET

SACRAMENTO STREET

Mozzarella di Bufala

BenéFit

PERINE PLACE

CALIFORNIA

STEINER STREET

Departures from the Past
Elite Café
Betsey Johnson

ORBEN PL

Harry's on Fillmore

STREET

200 Metres
200 Yards

PINE

Café Fiorio

Upper Haight

SHRADER STREET

COLE STREET

CLAYTON STREET

ASHBURY STREET

PAGE

PAGE

STREET

The Herb'N Inn
Great Expectations
Mansion

Mc Bodys

Martin Macks
Backseat Betty

HAIGHT

Aardvark's
Club Deluxe

The Pork Sto

The Citrus Club

The Booksmith
El Balazo
Westward
Villains

Zam
Zam

.1500

Cha Cha Cha

HAIGHT

Zona Rosa
The Red Vic
Ken Zaman

The Red Victorian Bed Breakfast and Art

Asqew Grill
Persian Aub Zam Zam

BELVEDERE STREET

CLAYTON STREET

ASHBURY STREET

WAL

Amoeba Records

SHRADER STREET

STREET

COLE STREET

WALLER STREET

DOWNEY STREET

STREET

DE

ST

ST

»

»

0 — 200 Metres

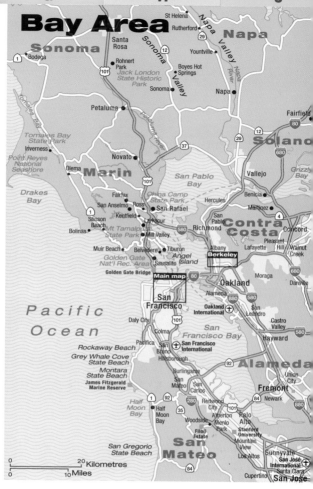

Bay Area

G   **H**   **J**

Sonoma   Napa   Solano   Marin   Contra Costa   Berkeley   Oakland   Alameda   San Mateo   San Jose

Pacific Ocean   San Francisco   San Francisco Bay

The East Bay

Getting there: The East Bay is linked to San Francisco via the underground BART transbay subway. Three lines run from Daly City through San Francisco and on to downtown Oakland, before diverging to service East Oakland. The AC Transit provides a good bus service around the entire East Bay area.

Attractions: Treasure Island; Oakland (downtown; Chinatown; Lake Merritt; Oakland Museum; the waterfront); Berkeley (University of California; Telegraph Avenue; Berkeley Marina; Six Flags Marine World; Mount Diablo State Park.

The Peninsula

Getting there: The BART travels down the Peninsula as far as Daly City, from where you can catch SamsTrans buses south to Palo Alto or along the coast to

Half Moon Bay. For longer distances Cal-Train offers an hourly rail service from its terminal at Fourth and Townsend streets (R9), stopping at most bayside towns between the city and San Jose. Greyhound runs regular buses along US-101 to and from their San Jose terminal.

Attractions: Palo Alto and Stanford University; San Jose and environs (San Jose Museum of Art, Tech Museum of Innovation; Children's Discovery Museum; Rosicrucian Museum; Winchester Mystery House; Paramount's Great America); James V. Fitzgerald Marine Reserve; Año Nuevo State Reserve.

Marin County

Getting there: ferries operate to Sausalito, Larkspur and Tiburon (*see Transport*). Golden Gate Transit also runs a comprehensive bus service around Marin from the Transbay Terminal (R6).

Attractions: Marin Headland; Sausalito; Muir and Stinson beaches; Point Reyes National Seashore; Mount Tamalpais State Park; Muir Woods National Monument; Mill Valley; Tiburon; Angel Island

The Wine Country

Getting there: a car is essential if you wish to explore the Wine Country (accessible by car from San Francisco in just over an hour). Golden Gate Transit run commuter buses every hour between Sonoma and Santa Rosa, while Greyhound has one bus daily to Napa and Sonoma from the Transbay Terminal (R6).

Attractions: Napa Valley wineries; St Helena; Calistoga spas; Robert Louis Stevenson Park; Sonoma Valley wineries; Jack London State Park; Russian River Valley.

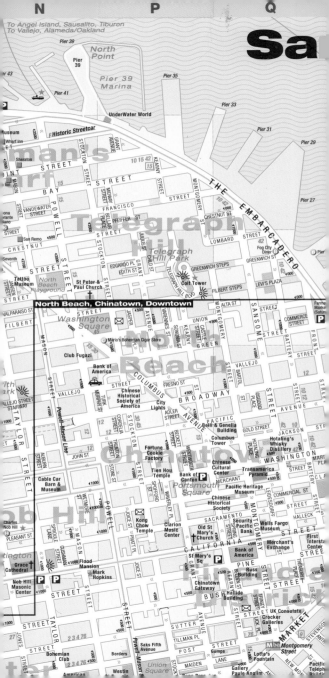

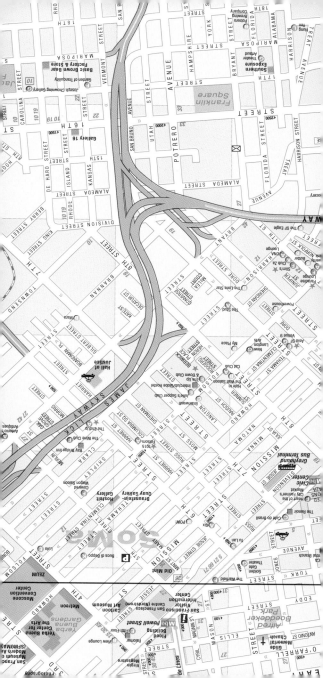

Mission-North

Intersection for the Arts 100 metres

Ti Couz
Clothes Contact
CALEDONIA ST
JULIAN STREET
WIESE STREET
16th Street Mission ◄3000
Theater Rhinoceros
The Lab
Truly Mediterranean
Ritmo Latino
The Roxie
The Dalva
The Albion

16TH STREET

Liquid

ALBION STREET

VALENCIA
500 ►
Bombay Bazar
Casanova
Slanted Door
Panchita's
Esta Noche
Pancho Villa
HOFF STREET
2000 ►
MISSION STREET
CAPP STREET
CAMP ST

17TH STREET

Murals
Thrift Town

CLARION ALLEY
Community Thrift
Country Station

0   100 Metres
0   100 Yards

Mary Elizabeth Inn   ◄1000

SUTTER
Red Room
Com Inter

John Pence Gallery
Boro
POST
Clarion Hotel

Alcazar Theatre

GEAR

Mission-South

Ruby Artists Cooperative Gallery
20TH   ST
La Rondalla
Encantada Galley of Fine Art
Retro Fit Vintage
VALENCIA
LEXINGTON STREET
SAN CARLOS ST
Andora Inn
MISSION

LIBERTY STREET

Artists' Television Access (ATA)
Herbivore

21ST   STREET
2500 ►

21ST   STREET
1000 ►
Lost Weekend Video
Firecracker
STREET
Rasoi
Dema
BARTLETT STREET
The Foreign Cinema
STREET

HILL STREET

The Marsh
Laku
The Lone Palm
Boogaloo's
Latin American Club
The Make-Out Room
Flying Saucer
22ND   STREET
Lucca Ravioli
Esperpento
22ND
STREET

0   100 Metres
0   100 Yards

LEAVENWORTH
O'FAR
◄500
EL
STREET
EDDY
S

G   H   J

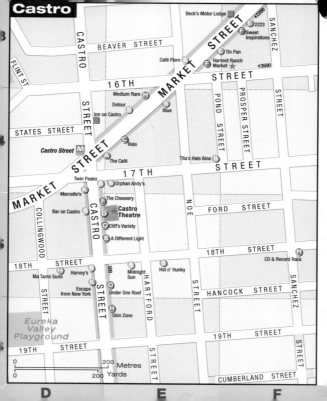

Castro

Beck's Motor Lodge

2223
Sweet Inspirations

CASTRO STREET

BEAVER STREET

MARKET STREET

Tin Pan

Café Flore

Harvest Ranch Market

SANCHEZ STREET

4200

3500

FLINT ST

16TH STREET

Medium Rare

Detour

Inn on Castro

Blue

CASTRO STREET

POND STREET

PROSPER STREET

STREET

STATES STREET

Castro Street

MARKET STREET

Rolo

The Café

Tita's Hale Aina

17TH STREET

Twin Peaks

Orphan Andy's

Marcello's

The Cheesery

Castro Theatre

Bar on Castro

Cliff's Variety

A Different Light

COLLINGWOOD

CASTRO STREET

NOE STREET

FORD STREET

18TH STREET

CD & Record Rack

SANCHEZ STREET

18TH STREET

Ma Tante Sumi

Harvey's

500

Midnight Sun

Hot n' Hunky

Escape from New York

Under One Roof

HARTFORD STREET

STREET

HANCOCK STREET

Skin Zone

Eureka Valley Playground

19TH STREET

19TH STREET

STREET

CUMBERLAND STREET

0   200 Metres
0   200 Yards

D   E   F

Sights

Berkeley Community Theater E9
California Memorial Stadium G9
Greek Theater G8
Judah L. Magnes Museum G10
Lawrence Hall of Science G8
University Art Museum F9
University of California F8
Valley Life Sciences F8

Hotels

Bancroft Hotel F9
Beau Sky Hotel F9
Berkeley City Club E9
Berkeley YMCA E9
Claremont Resort & Spa G10
Durant F9
Elmwood House F10
French E7
Golden Bear Motel B8

Gramma's Rose Garden Inn F10
The Shattuck E9
Travelodge D8

Streets

2nd–4th Streets	A7	Berkeley Way	C8	Claremont Avenue	G10
5th–10th Streets	B7	Berryman Street	E7	College Avenue	F10
Acton Street	C9	Blake Street	C9	Cornell Avenue	C7
Ada Street	C7	Bolivar Drive	A9	Curtis Street	C8
Addison Street	B9	Bonar Street	E9	Cyclotron Road	G8
Adeline Street	E10	Bonita Avenue	E8	Dane Street	F10
Allston Street	D9	Bowditch Street	F9	Deakin Street	E11
Allston Way	B9	Buena Avenue	D7	Delaware Street	B8
Alvarado Road	S4	Burnett Street	C10	Derby Street	C10
Anthony Street	B10	Byron Street	C9	Dohr Street	C10
Arch Street	E8	California Street	B7	Durant Avenue	E9
Ashby Avenue	D10	Camelia Street	B7	Dwight Way	C9
Avenida Drive	B9	Campus Drive	G7	Eastshore Frontage Road	A8
Bancroft Way	B9	Canyon Road	G9	Edith Street	D7
Belvedere Avenue	C7	Carleton Street	B10	Ellsworth Street	E10
Benvenue Avenue	F10	Carlotta Avenue	F10	Emerston Street	E11
		Cedar Street	B8	Etna Street	F10
		Centennial Drive	G9	Euclid Avenue	F7
		Center Street	E9	Fairlawn Drive	G7
		Channing Way	B9	Fernwald Road	G9
		Chaucer Street	B9	Forest Avenue	F10
		Chestnut Street	C8	Francisco Street	D8

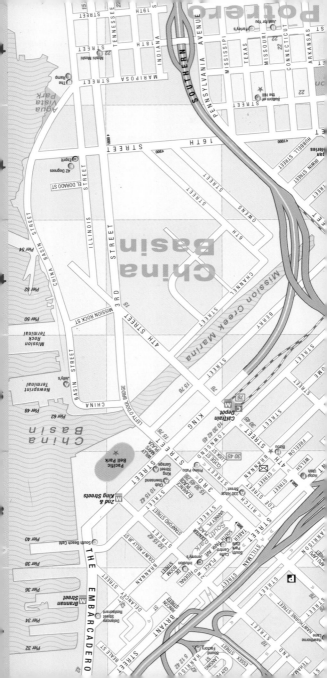

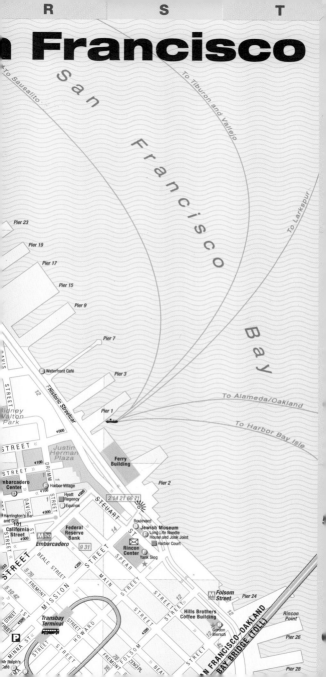

n Francisco

San

F r a n c i s c o

B a y

To Sausalito

To Tiburon and Vallejo

To Larkspur

Pier 23

Pier 19

Pier 17

Pier 15

Pier 9

Pier 7

Waterfront Café

Pier 3

To Alameda/Oakland

To Harbor Bay Isle

Historic Streetcar

12

Pier 1

Sidney
Walton
Park

Justin
Herman
Plaza

Ferry
Building

Pier 2

STREET

DRUMM

STREET

DAVIS

STREET

Embarcadero
Center

Harbor Village

Hyatt
Regency

Equinox

2 14 21 66 71

STEUART

ST

Boulevard

Jewish Museum
Long Life Noodle
House and Jook Joint

Harbor Court

Harrington's Bar
and Grill

101
California
Street

Federal
Reserve
Bank

M bq

Embarcadero

9 31

SPEAR

STREET

14

Rincon
Center

Yank Sing

California
Street

BEALE STREET

MISSION

STREET

MAIN

STREET

FREMONT

Folsom
Street

Pier 24

Rincon
Point

Hills Brothers
Coffee Building

Pier 26

Transbay
Terminal

HOWARD

STREET

FOLSOM

STREET

Gordon
Biersch

P

MINNA ST

Mr Ralph's
Café

BEALE

TEHAMA PL

ZENO PL

SAN FRANCISCO-OAKLAND
BAY BRIDGE (TOLL)

Pier 28

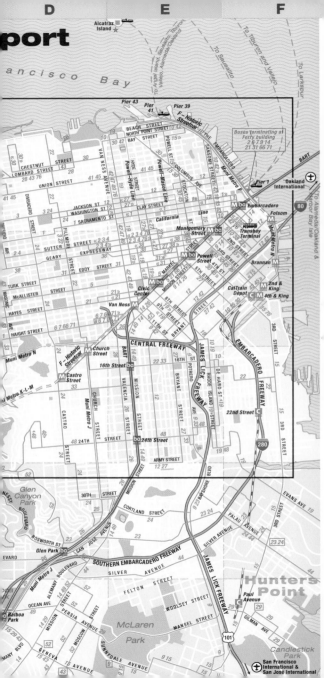

1

Golden Gate National
Recreation Area

San

Main map

101

GOLDEN GATE BRIDGE

2

The
Presidio

Baker
Beach

China
Beach

Lands
End

Lobos Creek
Valley

California Palace of
the Legion of Honor

Lincoln
Park

Yoshi's-san's Monkichi
20TH

Holy Virgin
Cathedral

Pacific
Café

CALIFORNIA

24

GEARY

3

Cliff
House
& Musée
Mécanique

Louis'
POINT LOBOS AVENUE

GEARY

BOULEVARD

Traktir

32ND

Trad' Sam's

La Vie

Khan
Toke

Ton
Kiang

Tommy's

Blarney
Stone

31 STREET

FULTON

Richmond

BALBOA

5 FULTON

STREET

Windmill
Beach Chalet

Golden ★ Gate Park

LINCOLN WAY

LINCOLN WAY

IRVING STREET

4

Ocean
Beach

Oceanview Motel

Muni Metro N

Java Beach
Café

Let It Be
Records

JUDAH

Marnee
Thai

PARNASSUS

LAWTON STREET

Sunset

NORIEGA STREET

BOULEVARD

QUINTARA STREET

Forest
Hill

WOODS

Muni Metro L

TARAVAL STREET

Parkside

Sunset
Motel

West
Portal

PORTOLA
DRIVE

5

Ocean
Park Motel

VICENTE STREET

Pine Lake
Park

Stern
Grove

SLOAT BOULEVARD

OCEAN AVENUE

San Francisco
Zoo

Stonestown

Muni Metro K

OCEAN AVENUE

Muni Metro M

GRAFTON

Harding
Park

Fort Funston

6

BROTHERHOOD

RANDOLPH STREET

LAKEVIEW AVE

Inglesid

WAY

Pacific Ocean

Coastal Trail

GREAT HIGHWAY

0   2 Kilometres
0   1 Miles

San Francisco
Golf Club

Street Index

Map labels (streets and locations):

Pyramid Brewery · STREET · Lalime's
GILMAN · 924 Gilman · Ashkenaz · KAINS · STANNAGE · TALBOT · AVE · CURTIS · SANTA FE AVENUE · NEILSON · NORTHSIDE · PERALTA AVENUE · GILMAN STR
4TH · 5TH · 6TH · 8TH · Picante · Narain's
CAMELIA · STREET
PAGE · STREET · JONES · ST · AVENUE · HOPKINS · CURTIS · BELVEDERE AVE · ROSE
CEDAR · STREET · Café Fanny · CEDAR · KAINS AVE · STANNAGE AVE · STRE
Golden Bear Motel · SAN · FRANKLIN
VIRGINIA · STREET · Café Rouge · Bel
Bette's Ocean View Diner
Hear Music · DELAWARE · STREET · HEARST · CURTIS · CHESTNUT · AVENUE
O Chame · East Bay Vivarium · BERKELEY
HEARST · AVENUE · 51 · UNIVERSITY
P · Spenger's
Freight and Salvage
Brennan's · PABLO
ADDISON · STREET · BONAR · STREE
Takara Sake USA
ALLSTON · WAY · Vik's Chat Corner · CURTIS · NOBAR · ACTON
BANCROFT · AVENUE · WAY · WEST · VALLEY · ACTO
4TH · 5TH · 6TH · 7TH · CHAUCER · STREET
CHANNING · WAY
EASTSHORE FRONTAGE ROAD · WEST FRONTAGE ROAD · BOLIVAR DRIVE · SEAWALL DRIVE · UNIVERSITY AVE · UNIVERSITY AVENUE
DWIGHT
BLAKE · STREET
7TH · 8TH · 10TH · PARKER · STREET · MATHEWS · PARKER
80 · CARLETON · STREET · CARLETON
Juan's Place · DERBY
PARDEE · STREET · WARD
GRAYSON · STREET · San Pablo Park · WALLACE · MABEL · PARK
HEINZ · STREET · RUSSEL · STREET
ANTHONY · STREET · BURNETT · STREET
POTTER · STREET

Transport

Getting around San Francisco is best done on foot as the city centre is compact. The hills, however, can be tiring, so consider the occasional flat – if less direct – route. The city's public transport system, Muni, covers every neighbourhood with its efficient system of cable cars, buses, trolleys and metro. But if you're taking a trip out of town, consider renting a car as public transport is infrequent and complicated.

From San Francisco International Airport

San Francisco International Airport (SFO) is located 15 miles south of the city. The quickest and most convenient option in to the city centre is the SFO Airporter bus, which costs $10 and picks up outside each baggage reclaim area every 15 minutes, travelling to Union Square (P6) and the Financial District (Q5) in about 30 minutes. The Supershuttle, American Airporter Shuttle and the Yellow Airport Shuttle minibuses offer a similar service, departing every five minutes from the upper level of the circular road and taking passengers to city centre destinations for around $12 a head. Taxis cost around $30 to any downtown destination and there are also numerous buses departing every half hour from the upper level of the airport to various destinations.

Muni buses, trolleys, metro & cable cars

The city's public transportation is run by the San Francisco Municipal Railway, or Muni. Muni comprises a comprehensive network of buses, trolleys, cable cars and six metro lines.

tickets

The flat fare on buses and trains is $1 (exact change only); you can ask for a free transfer with each ticket you buy. Cable cars cost $2 one-way and do not accept transfers. If you plan on riding the cable car more than once, pick up a one-day Muni Passport ($6) from the Visitor Center. The passport is valid for unlimited travel on the Muni system, including cable cars and BART stations within the city limits. The passport is also available in three-day and seven-day denominations. A Fast Pass costs only $9 a week but excludes cable cars, though the $35 pass (valid for a full calender month) includes unlimited transportation on these historic vehicles.

Bay Area Rapid Transit (BART & CalTrain

Five BART routes provide the fastest way to get to the East Bay and the suburbs east and south of the city tre. BART shares a station with Muni along Market S (Q6) downtown.

The CalTrain commuter railway (depot at Fourth and Townsend, SoMa; R9) links San Francisco with San Jose.

Ferries

Golden Gate Ferries leave from the Ferry Building (S crossing the bay to Sausalito (H3) and Larkspur (H2 Blue & Gold Fleet sails from Pier 41 (N1) to Sausalito Tiburon (H3). The Alameda-Oakland ferry sails betwe Fisherman's Wharf (N1), the Ferry Building (S4) and Oakland's Jack London Square.

Taxis

Cabs ply the streets, but finding an available taxi car difficult. Hail one in the street or try Veterans (415/55 1300) or Yellow Cab (415/626-2345).

Driving & cycling

The only reason to rent a car in San Francisco is to explore the Bay Area beyond the city. The California Department of Transport (CalTrans) operates a toll-fre hour information line (1-800/427-ROAD) giving up-to minute details of road conditions throughout the state

The big international car-rental firms have outlets at airport and downtown, all have various rates and spe offers. Dollar (415/771-5300) and Reliable (415/928-4414) are at the cheaper end of the spectrum. Other Francisco offices include Alamo (415/882-9440), Avis (415/885-5011), City-Rent-a-Car (415/861-1312), Enterprise (15/441-3369), Hertz (415/771-2200) and Thrifty (415/788-8111).

Cycling is a good way of getting around town. There a marked bike routes to all major points of interest. For rental try Park Cyclery (1749 Waller Street; 415/751-7

Scootcar Rentals (M2) rent out motorized buggies for entertaining, self-guided whizz around the city.

Sights

Hotels